Visions of the Manifestations Poetically Speaking to One

THE VISION

Jacquelyn Rice Dunbar

authorHOUSE®

AuthorHouse™
1663 Liberty Drive
Bloomington, IN 47403
www.authorhouse.com
Phone: 1-800-839-8640

First published by AuthorHouse 3/18/2010

ISBN: 978-1-4490-5627-8 (e)
ISBN: 978-1-4490-5625-4 (sc)

Library of Congress Control Number: 2010902033

Printed in the United States of America
Bloomington, Indiana

This book is printed on acid-free paper.

Contents

Autobiography 1

"A thorn in My Side" 2

All around thee...3

Another Year...4

Bare Skin..5

Being Thankful 6

Caught In the Rapture...7

Character of One 8

Closure to One...9

"Discomfort Joy" 10

Don't Live in Regrets 11

Don't Walk Away 12

"Elegance of One" 13

Father Versus Daddy 14

"A Final Breath" 15

"For the Moment" 16

Forgiveness of One 17

Fractional Frictions of One 18

Free in Thee...19

From Where I Came From 20

Full Circle..21

Get a Grip..22

Grandmother 23

How did I get to this Place..24

Humble Thee 25

I am sorry I cant Accompany You 26

I Gave my Best 27

I was just Checking 28

Interest Free 29

Living Each Day 30

Living in the Past 31

Love Blindly Shattered 32

Love Me For Me 33

Mistress...34

"My Fathers Eye" 35

My Friend For Life 36

My Inside Soul 37

"My Little Girl" 38

My Mothers Voice 39

Never Changing 40

No Time Like Today 41

"Not A Child of Mine" 42

Nothing But Success 43

Optimistic..44

Passion of One 45

Please Come Rescue Me 46

Priorities of One 47

Puzzling Pieces 48

Reconnected 49

Reconstruction Mentally 50

Reflections 51

Reserved 52

Resolution...53

"Rise Above Thee" 54

Romantic Dinner 55

"Running Inside of Me" 56

A Scorned Woman 57

Seasonal Changes...58

Shadows of the Unknown...59

Sheltered Life 60

Standing Alone 61

Standing Ovation 62

Substitution...63

Teddy Bears 64

"The Twin I never Knew" 65

The Vision 66

"The Wife of Mine" 67

"The World Owes You Nothing" 68

There is No Tomorrow 69

Three Sides of the Story..70

Triumphs..71

Trouble Makers 72

Unexpected 73

Well Beyond..74

What Came Over Me...75

What is your Given Purpose 76

What Keeps me Going...77

What Point Are You At 78

What to Believe..79

Why Are you in Questioning 80

Why are you so Cold to Me 81

Special Thanks...83

Autobiography

I am thankful for everything god has stored upon me and I take nothing for granted, because, I know it didn't have to be so.

I am the proud mother of 3 beautiful children, Diamond, Desmond, & Destiny. I am the wife of Robert Wayne Dunbar.

I am the daughter of Bennie & Cynthia Rice. As well as Shirley Henderson (Second Mother)

My siblings are Bennie L. Rice,(Jacqueline), Latarsha Benton(Michael), Lakaye Cheek, & (Best friend/Sister), Jillian Davenport (Kevin).

I was born and raised here in Greensboro, NC & love it with a passion as well as writing poetry. I am currently studying journalism on the campus of Guilford Technical College here , in Greensboro. I am excited to new endeavors, where god is going to take me next..

"A thorn in My Side"

The ways of the people of the world, planted a depth of sadness inside

You tried in many ways, to strip me of my innocence, but my heavenly father would not allow this will to be done…

For, I have carried this burden with me for many years to come, but you my heavenly father knew all along A thorn in my side, has been removed, all at once….

2

All around thee

As I awaked to the manifestation creations …I remained silent, just in sweet meditation of all around thee, birds of such eagle dreams made whole in me…Not a day that passes me, that I am not satisfied with the cause of thee…For all I know is that he restored my soul in order for me to be bought forth into his promises already predestined for me… Even when I thought I was all alone, you showed up to carry me on where I was feeling all apart…However, he's there all around thee….

Another Year

Countless to say we have somehow and someway encountered
another year in significant way…So many we witnessed, being
called on home to thee…Of course, this brought about a conversional
emotions running un tamed within thee…Leaving all kinds of
emotions, confused, on where to go from here, no one knows…It was
then that, an angel whispered in such a round about way…Go on and
know I got you covered from the nearest sow…Another year, never
truly promised but hoped to be for thee…Another year , Another
Year, oh what a blessing this is to hear quite mordacious indeed…
Thanking god , you spared my life , for another year to thee…

Bare Skin

The creation of a woman's bare is a rare….Taken the rib bones from man to help make woman to be fully desirable to thee… Bare Skin, Bare Skin, Bare Skin…The body linings of her uniqueness curves that helped mold her to her own special way….Its natural beauty stood out on its own in its entirety in a very special way….

Being Thankful

Another day gifted with air ….

Doing well with my right mind to only look around to see everything you have created for me…

It was the bigger miracles that left me so amazed of your wondrous ways you perform each and everyday..

I am thankful , for my friends that remain & family that came to beckon call when in despair … Being thankful , is not always what some feel meaning, your emotions may take you ever which way… Just knowing you give me that inner strength to keep on pressing my way….

So I give much gratitude in everyway & saying thanks in a very special way, for thinking to create me with its uniqueness in everyway……

Caught In the Rapture

So many illusions of what was expected in collusive of thee…

Time running frivolously…No determination of departing this decisive rig amour indeed….

Never thought past, the first distinction of the impressive impression you left with me….You lured me in like the fisherman's bait…I must admit, he was a catch to fitting to me…The charm of your every notional wit , in hopes for a close knit in capture …I felt your reservoir, as you sought out me in every minute given….Seemed like something unrealistically never imagined before….

The Rapture has me held captive in a sum….

Character of One

Characteristically, speaking is what will and can make ones appearance to others of one…

Ones developmentally, historically from day one to now…What did you learn , what did you do, and what did you speak of throughout ones journey 's life to this day in every which way…Character of one, determining who and what you will overall end up to be…

Closure to One

While running your life like the marathon race that you were obviously in it to win…. Never really giving ones soul time to bring to a halt to the previous …How could you devour all of self to a second one , when the first has not even been brought to a head all in one… Too many things happened all at once, with no sense of organization or yet agenda of any or one….Stop being in a hurry, to began another without giving yourself time to ponder… Closure of one, eliminates all the excessive baggage that may be accompanied in one….

"Discomfort Joy"

At some point & time we all have been feeling guilt, shame, hurt that has left us displaced…

Bringing on numerous emotions that are untamed ….

Brought on by the expectations of this place of the world..

Looking for gratitude in things & persons laird. .No satisfaction, received, just grief of what they expected of me…

Never once seeking gods permission to leave the peaceful place…

For the promise of discomfort joy, was created by evil Sayers envoy…

Discomfort Joy, has been made acceptable amongst most, who would dare to enjoy…For life & jeopardy would soon bewildered if you didn't take the interest to explore…

Don't Live in Regrets

So many opportunities wished for & hoped for, but never sought the fight to grab hold to it...

I could turn the times back, I would embrace every opportunity that would elevate me to the next big success ...

If there was a intuition to follow through, don't under estimate the thought but better equip self to what is required in you , to do you ....Live everyday , for if it was your last... So take hold to opportunities now, for they may not come back just for you...

A lot of wish I could oaf's and should of 's, but no I did do's.....Put yourself out there, into the unfamiliar zone.....

Don't Walk Away

For there are still unfinished cares left in the air…

Don't walk away, for I never expressed my gratitude of your love you conveyed repetitiously to thee…

For everything you have shown, never went un noticed to me…I need you , I need you , to be my shining light with the armor in the night ….You were more hero, for I cherished every second with thee , for all we know It could be our last….So lets hit replay, the image of us in dire bare happiness like once before…

Don't walk away , for I never want to say my good byes, so I say until we meet again my sweet…

"Elegance of One"

As you sit there like you were on the finest jet magazine cover ready to pose, It took no artificial coloring of ones outer being, just your mere natural beauty glowed as if you only knew....It was spontaneous, like the perfect picture you could snap from a Kodak make... You appeared stunning, as there was a view of astonishment...Not, to say, you could never appear in this way, but there was nothing that equipped me for what I would say....Oh my, your extravagant glare caught me across the room as there I dared to stare....Elegance of one, was captivating to one....

Father Versus Daddy

A Father Is a Man, who has his named signed on the line, of one who which he aided,

In the creative self being… Does this really mean, he has it in him to be the man he was originated to be…Leaving me the resolution that he would meet the part he set out to be…

Another male , that took part in the completion of that beautiful creation the other sought out to be…

A daddy, is just that one, that contributed has seed to bring life but not to finish what was started to the light …

"A Final Breath"

Afflictions hit heavenly upon ones breast, with no righteous cure, not now nor ever…

Life's natural elements that wore one down, no where to turn, one displaced in thy head…

One began again, to speak what was churning in the head, cries of endless endeavors never turning around for the better instead failing amongst the dead..

Just couldn't make sense of all that was taken place, just condensed immensely over ones head…

One knew this was the final scene, where you waited for someone to come rescue thee.. No one came, not a sunder came close to this mended bed…

As one once again gasped for the final greed, silence feel keen to the ground, as it was spoken with such dire despair, It was better to love than to love one, as one dropped its head…

"For the Moment"

For this moment, It was clear to thee, of the feeling I immensely felt for thee...

You questioned, the emotion like it was a mere dream that would soon vanish into the listening skies..

Was implausible, of what await me on the following day that was to follow...

So, I ceased the moment for tomorrow was only hoped for, but not promised ...

I was living the moment like no other, for I knew this would soon too pass...

Never wanting it to come to a halt, but surely I was acting frivolously of what time was allotted with thee... For the moment, I will love you fearlessly, in such a way it would be memorable to thee...

Forgiveness of One

We all struggle from day to day with that hanging burden, that we have allowed to stay…

Others, have gone on to the next, while we have charged our self with this confinement..

Couldn't seem to shake this forever feeling that has seemly taken control of you in every way…

After the fall, it has become time to stand back up with a different insight of where to go next..

For everything, has a place & reasoning in which it happened this way….Lords know, I am only human, like others around me, but because I set the expectations on a tremendous high that took me stumbling on the edge of time….I reclaimed everything that was once lost in another life time, for this is a new day, for possibilities to continue on in a more positive way… Forgiveness of one, is continuing process, of ones true confessions day in and out upon one….

Fractional Frictions of One

Too much and too little to say , for there is always an excuse being acknowledged in various ways..

No, true indication, that there was a liking of one….Always, some drama, giving way to the optimistic laical theory of one….So much lingering & making itself right at home, it has plum wore its welcome out in what it called itself home…Fractional Frictions, when you intertwine the two, you get even a bigger mess than the past one….

Free in Thee

Carefree of correlation, that tried to take over thee…No reasonable doubt to second guest what was to be…

I take things as they come, one by one….Leaving room for improvement of trial in error in yesterday's that has already come…I am free indeed, my mind going outrageously fast pace in everyway… No time to slow it down, for I have people to see & places to make myself known….

From Where I Came From

I came from the mere dust particles created by our highly father who sits high and sits low…

Dust to dust and ashes to ashes as I depart this temporary soul….

Came from little, and made due to get to the next…

It was like a miracle that I would soon to unfold…..Not much I say, but thankful anyway….But much plentiful I would say each and everyday….Sometimes, I hoped for a little more, then I use discernment on what I thought I could not bare without ….

For when the time would come & surely it would be soon …..I would give back to who helped me to be what I am now & later, from where I came from….From where I came from…is never to be forgotten….

Full Circle

Starting with box one, then the next, & only to the last like never before…

There was a gray mist neither here nor there to wither…Indecisive, with the directional points to go on…

Round and Round, with the wheels spinning out a control in a dire hole…

Full Circle, Full Circle, it goes to say be careful what you partake from the then to the now…

Compelling the beginning to the detouring the end…

Get a Grip

Things being tossed here and there…No wander you looked with such a dare, of what to do…. You fell into insanity to be exact ..Troubling some , of who or what you were…Get a grip of reality, for you go Snapple pop….Get a grip to life's mishaps, that will corrupt your living energies if allotted in this ridiculous way…Get a grip to things of truths with meaning in one's heart being…

Grandmother

She catered to us like we had special maid service in everyway…

She cooked all those goodies with an extra special love….She loved me
extra when no one else was near… I missed her sweet little voice, that
always comforted my inner securities within the depths of my soul
until she was laid to rest in the very end…

How did I get to this Place

Here, I stood so still and no way to just get away ... How did I get to
this place, where everyone looked out for self... No one ever really
cared about why some people cried or even why some were so glad....
Some jobless leaving them hopeless of what tomorrow holds......
Children dying from starvation across our nations with no means
investing souls to bring better days , giving someone else;' s soul the
enlighten peace in knowing someone truly cared...No one has the time
or really priority ones mind set to the test, to put another first .....How
did I get to this Place, we forget to consider others....

Humble Thee

One's delightful movement, that would forever leave such an
impressive impression of one…

The meekness, the tenderness and at ease to go on to what was next…

Not one to have kept confusion, but, of much peace to be sung
amongst others that would come…

Such a delicate manner, in which was shown from the inner soul…

Some, may have taken it for a weakness and others for what it was…
Kindness and sweetness that lived within one's heart..

Humble thee, Humble thee, Humble thee, where nature's peace
dwelled indeed…

I am sorry I cant Accompany You

I am sorry , I cant accompany you, I am sorry I have a call on me, by god himself to do right and nothing in between…

I am sorry, my change puts you in a different prospective towards me…

I am sorry you find yourself saying, I just wont be bend any to thee…

I am sorry you feel as if this is just a game towards you…

Let the truth be told, this sudden call would either make or break us …

I am sorry you try not to give govern to what has been told…I say I want be accompany you to this peak….

I Gave my Best

I set out with the mindset to give my all & do my best…

With the determination that I would not walk away from thee..

Knowledgeable, of the possibility of failing & even given way of soaring in gratitude of a success…I gave my best, from start to finish, clearing my conscience that I did run through the hoops of life and aim for one thing only, my best , given my best is all I told…

I was just Checking

Have not talked to you in a while…What have I missed from one's
inner piece my dear…

What new journey 's have you, sought out since our last conversation
What is the driven force behind your daily course of action….I was just
checking, I was just checking, to see if you were fine indeed…

Interest Free

Unlike, our everyday plastics that we swipe quite frequently….It gives one a sense of over the top living, so many thought forever more….. Needless to say, it was a sudden resolution in regards to what the world offered to you… However, many had a slight oversight of this over sized promotion throughout the year for only thee…

It gives you back more than a 30 day back guarantee, it is lifetime of peace, love, & joy passing all understanding, that lives eternity..

Highly recommended with 100% satisfaction for all regardless of your credit ratings or even quota status amongst us all here indeed…This brings a delightful relief for millions… that there is a Interest Free, the offer of God to thee….

Living Each Day

Each day is a fresh of newness coming ones way…Never know, what trial may face you in this given day…There may be one, or many, but just tackle one by one…

You are only human, so the fleshly could relay in a different formally in a tedious way…Even though challenges come in numerous sizes, some may be bigger than you, so what do in this un predictable day..

No one knows the hour or nor the second that the father that sits high & low, will follow his endowing notions to come get you & take you back with him, a peaceful home.. Living Each day, with appreciation of every miracle that has been & will be performed in given day in which we take a part of in every way…Living Each day , in progress, to improving the betterment of one in its rarity to some….

Living in the Past

If you are constantly dwelling on what has happened or didn't happen in the past, you will never truly enjoy what is in the present or furthermore in the days to come....Don't count them as loses, but gains to what lies ahead you in just moments to come....

Love Blindly Shattered

As I watched him mingle with people of his own status in life..

It broke me down , leaving me distorted within thee…

He never knew the emptiness that came rapidly over thee, as I observed him ravishing another over me…

As the tears poured down, I knew this would rapture me…

No one to love, kiss, hold, or captivate my body in a whole…

Lost inside & out , no where to go , no where to hide, just silence of the pain that I cared to bury within me…

Long sighs for moments at a time, contemplating suicide in me…

Never placing no one before him, but my mother…Sad to say, I confided immensely in a wrong …Did I love him, Oh yes, excessively No time allotted for friends, I would say…Just me & my boo in every descriptive way…

Things were soon to change, that is no boo in my way, from the realness that stood right over there awaiting just for me…

Love Me For Me

I had never asked much of you not one single second time…

No one took time to study me inside and out…Just making assumptions, of what you thought to be factual but not really actual…

I was somewhat disturbed by your ignorance you utterly demonstrated repetitiously….

For the little girl inside of me fought to find a place inside you….

Reluctantly, to say I was lost without a single mention of what it was to me inside & out….

The residue of your substitutions, that just want do, It is me and only me….I advised you frivolously, don't attempt to convert me to your special image that never existed ….Why cant you just love me for me and stay contempt with what is bestowed upon you , neither more, nor less…..So love me for me…..

Mistress

So many nights I laid alone, without the simple touch of one…

Your time seemed preoccupied with another standing there in your way…

What to do, I stood there waiting for thee to return to thee..

Only, to still feel the emptiness from the depth inside, of just knowing you were just a temporary fantasy, that would leave me vulnerable & hurt…

I asked the mere question why, did you come by, and shine your light of passion from inside…

You, were left with the speechless face that became un bearable to this side…..

"My Fathers Eye"

My Fathers eye never left my side, as I flickered an eye…

He always would forewarn me of unseen dangers that lied ahead…

For the words he knew, would some how make me feel safe inside…

He would sacrifice his own safety so that I might be free of mine…

I admired him, for such great compassion he wildered inside…For all my hurt incurred, he wiped them away with a twinkle of an eye..

My fathers eye, could never be replaced for another …

For I will always love you father for everything you are & will be from this day forward…

My Friend For Life

A friend for life is someone , who appears in the rare…Never too busy, never uneasy to what you may have to share….Surely when you are in wrong, they just look & stare….Not always, in agreeing with what you had to clear the air….Letting you finish, with their lips closed shut, then softly mutter a slight sigh….Looking to you with the question, now what do you dare to do, for your own inner being will guide you to the true….Not really, what you wished or hoped to hear, but they just knew you would do what made them feel at peace in their heart…. My friend for life, My friend for life, will never change nor vanish in anyway…..

My Inside Soul

My inside soul, is full, of so much anguish placed inside, from those who misused and abused your mold..

My inside soul holds a genuine love with compassion too, for most, I could ever meet…I guess you could say, I would be caught, with my heart hanging on its way…My inside soul, also, has a low point of tolerance to dwell…Could leave a despair of depression, when things get really rough & tough to bare…

Most of all, My inside soul is never to extend too thin in its lightness in the air…

"My Little Girl"

She appeared, like such an angel piece loved tremendously..

I would take great aptitude, in what she would dare to wear..

She grew like the blossom of breath taken flowers you would see during the warmth air…

My little girl, could relinquish her mind and soul right into the palm of my hand …

My little girl, so undeceive like her mother said…

My Mothers Voice

As she Laid in her bed, there was a low pitch voice that whispered to me...Please come and be here with me...

She heard her cry for someone to be by her side which immediate attention upon her call...

My mothers voice called her constantly day in & day out, vulnerable for that love like no other shown to me before...

Never Changing

Feeling the sense of the urge to be no other way but me from the top to the bottom.. Feeling me to the fullest, A new sexy attitude with class to observe …Never , easily persuaded by others poor choices or in words…Never Changing, to the occasion, but changing so I represent me…Content with just being me and only me….Never cared to switch but modified the gratified of your own pride in joy …

I choice to live one day at a time & live with no regrets of changing the way I was originated to be….

No Time Like Today

No time like today, so why do you allow things to stand in your way…
Why are you so persistent in following this way…For you never
know, tomorrow may not ever come your way…Leave room for you
to follow through on every desire in this special day …No time like
today, for all those things you wish you had said or even not said…..
Live in short forgiveness, so you can move on to other assignments
that easily come unexpected to you on the next & even the day after….
Do all you can do until your body replies to you, you can stop now &
pick up where it follows for the next day if it follows….

"Not A Child of Mine"

How could you send me away, lost in a moment of time..

It brought shame to you in every vindictive way….

You never made mention of me to your acquaintances that crossed
your path..

It was never clear to me, what distort thee…

It was like the newness of a toy & soon to be worn off..

I was like your reflection in a mirror, in this lifetime..

For, you are still in displace, of how I came to this place…

You refused to man up, no babies here, no babies here, I could hear
you ringing in my ears like the sparkles of stars in one…

For my spirit, will forever live on from this day on…

Nothing But Success

I don't have to have an audience to go further than the last and to succeed indeed…I am my own motivator!!! Nothing but success here….Nothing but success here…

Optimistic

Many opportunities, coming to you from previous closures allured before..

No time like the present, for time is of the essence to all …Optimistic, is the thinking the well beyond & further in time, for things you are now placing in line….Nothing wrong, with this mind setting in line, for all you know, you could be the next multi million dollar winning proceeds…

Passion of One

A burning desire for more, more, A burning desire for more, For what fills your inner being, it pours out as you soar through this journey of opportunities for even more…. Passion, Passion, Passion, is felt in the depth of my soul, for when I look out to the crowds, I see only the lights of its glow that completes me in a very special way….So live it and dare to go further than the last and embrace your passion of one …..

Please Come Rescue Me

Please, come rescue me from all the painful things that lay around and even inside me… I once was lost in the damnation of this world, no one never knew that thy inner soul was burning, with shattered pieces falling where they may…

There were bandages relinquishing in these empty places, hoping to regain the triumph of the slandering words once spoken of to me….

I had been rid curried, of such impulsive actions taken from him before….No more, No more, I say, will I stand for such throat cutting words to hinder my obsession with the righteous before me….Rescue me, Rescue me, & take me to a safe haven , where no one can touch thee….

Priorities of One

First and foremost, I give my gratitude of appreciation to my heavenly father who took time to create me…For whom knows my every desire and hears my every cry…Then my families well being standing there in the forefront in thee eye….My Special interest of one came so conclusive to thee…

The passions of one's hopes come from the depths within…Priorities of one, must keep from being detangled in thee….

Puzzling Pieces

There I stood still in a discerned stare…Nothing seemly fit in life's unexpected crystallized events, that somehow would lose its molding fit… Never giving up & never giving in to those life's bazaar devastations as they unfold before me … Seemly, not fair, but you take your loses and move on to your next assignment that you dare…

I simply maneuvered, everything's arrangement that stood in my way, so that I could arrive at my determined destination in the set out way…

Everything finally fitting in its rightful places that once was in array of shattered pieces …Puzzling Pieces, have found their prospective places & now I can say all my aspirations have created the inner happiness in this way…

Reconnected

Joined together from the hip to the bone....Never leaving one side to be all alone...Reconnected to the mental being & hopefully joining one's heart in thee... We missed so much time, But now we back amongst thee...Never wishing to depart from thee...For we intertwine with each others souls in one complete whole...Reconnected, the basic intercession of love for another & a complete unfold unconditionally in this magnificent way that I willingly display.... Not ashamed of what recreated from the previous life time, but just breath taken, of the what was & now what is lingering there....

Reconstruction Mentally

It is your own thought, that determines what is to come next…
Positively, the prognosis, gives a mortifying of hope & faith in which
despair is still there… When it comes to what you believe, this will
conduct the crystallized results to the end…

Reflections

So many times, we blamelessly, find fault in all others…Never truly depicting on self…Mirror , Mirror on the wall you are immoralist of them all…Reflections, Reflections, Reflections, are one's Flawless flaws inaudibly….

No real time to reflect on mine; for your attention lies elsewhere at this moment in time….Reflections, reflections, Reflections, of the one true divine…..Take a long stare in the mirror and you will soon become aware it is your reflection, that stares you down from this and there….

Reserved

I sat in silence, as I observed what was & going to take its place….

Never one to say much, until there was burning desire to be…

Not one of a lot of here Sayers comments, just moving my Mosley way…

I listened cautiously to ones voice & emphasis in one…Not truly interested in what I assumed to had heard, but more so to what was not to say….Sometimes, it was not what one has said, but what was not mentioned earlier, you know the lines that lie between ….Surely it was an oversight on their part they would hoped that you would say, but I was much too smart for this kind of mental play…..I stay reserved, for no one knows what I hold or what would get told….

Resolution

At some point in ones life, there are intentional agendas put in place to
follow up in their own designated way....Some commitments meant to
keep & some went astray, for all were intended to stay ...Resolution,
a requisition displaced in a certain way....Truly it takes a tremendous
amount of effort to bring a conclusive resolution to it all... Resolution,
Resolution, lets make a mends to this so uncultivated end...

"Rise Above Thee"

As my life drowned underneath the sand, seemly no sound could be heard…

Circumstances burdensome, that there was no air flowing through me, but the anchor hindered me…

There was a sense of guilt, shame, and defeat, but It was known of the wondrous endeavors sent from above…

I rose with the confidence of knowing I could go on to be whatever I wanted to be…

Romantic Dinner

For the evening was set for only real lovers near…

Candles lit from the door to the resting room of amour…

Roses, slightly cut fitting like the crêpes on beautiful drapes nicely displayed…

As you laid there looking like freshness I enjoy…

You aroused my inner being, from the beginning to the end…

Table preset for two for the occasional event that was to take place..

Excitement brought forth, of the unknown of what I anticipated from thence moment to the next…

It was an experimental arousing your sexual stimulation to explode…

Hearing the explosive magical sparks fall where they may never told…

I felt your energy as you transferred to lured me within… A night of various events never -ending performance, that overlaid its imagining light …..

"Running Inside of Me"

So many flaws to live up to, so many mistakes I ran into….

Ideas, theories running rapidly inside out & outside in….

The gumption to attempt to compete against this thing or something
that was soon to explode…Everything came on me all at once….

I attempted to juggle this, that, all, & only to recover the pain that
lie in the fore front of me…Like the tedious winds of a tornado
storm…Going full speed ahead, without the possibility of ceasing or
serenading in these triumphs soon to come….

Out of order as can be, running inside of me, running inside me, the
issues that resurfaced themselves all over me….

I felt as if someone had conquered over me, repetitiously….

Running inside of me, running inside of me, I cant let this get the best
of me….

A Scorned Woman

Repetitiously beat, with the words of slander to thee…. She felt as if she could not leave thee..

Weakness feel upon one body leaving her feeling an affliction of the illness to me…

Your hands over taken thee, you dragged me down aisles, bruised thy face, relinquishing the beauty that god gifted me …..Friends fore warned thee, but there was a stubbornness that stuck to thee…Many wondered would she overcome the power of self beauty in one or would she vanish in distorted form…

A Scorned Woman, A Scorned Woman, there is hope for the many in one…..

Seasonal Changes

There are numerous life changing events that take us in a snare, some breaking us down, some uplift our souls, some manifest the unfold, some shed life on what you already knew, some bring the importance of life itself to the fore front......Changing seasons, are like the airs in which we breathe, some feeling fair & others you feel you cant even bare.....

Shadows of the Unknown

I awake from my sleep, to this image of something or someone looking over me....At first I grew in fret of what was coming over me....

Nothing, of the normal, I convinced myself, over and over...

Then I remembered my grandmother's sweet ole voice, lecturing me of life's misfortunes & precious I guard you for the rest of your life...

I had no beliefs of such, but believed that her spirit may be killed but, her lively spirit of life beyond soared through my unknown zone...

It was that shadow of the unknown to others , that I spoke of this to....

Surely, I was not going delirious or even frivolously of what I saw or even felt...

Let the truth be told, her spirit lived in the depth my heart that could & would never depart....

Shadows of the unknown, make yourself loud and known for those that live on self reliance alone.....

Sheltered Life

The world surrounds us with its extremes that are rather
extraordinaire to me …

Things seem crystal perfect through these eyes on me…Nothing out
of its place, just peace & happiness in its rightful place…Now, come
here, is this realistic to think that life is so perfect with no flaws near…
No knowledge of what it is to do without, just what it is to be with, is
all I knew my dear…Sheltered life, Sheltered life, or what a false image
being painted of what the world lob to thee….It would have been
absolute false tense surrounding thee….

Standing Alone

Sometimes you may seemly find yourself standing alone, when others around you don't understand you....Be strong and keep pressing your way to your destination...Even, if there are things in such array, tell them firmly move out of your way!!! I have places to go and people to see....

Standing Ovation

Lights, camera, and action, ready to begin…

What seemed a halt to the end…

What an action filled show, that left millions enclosed… Fearful, from the start, of everyone's reaction in such a delight … The aim was to bring a delight pleasure, to attract the spotlight all in all… There came at the finality a standing ovation…People, were refigured on what people could see, the quietness & meekness of thee…Bravo, Bravo, Bravo, what a standing ovation it was, the crowds standing with astonishment at the end….

Substitution

So many times, we find ourselves leaning towards, what the world has so conveyed in this world….

We looked to what we felt would alleviate the inner sufferings we endured inside…

Substitution , Is what some would call it & others would convey it a comfort zone…

Many setbacks, from what we sought to come… Many excuses, for many take for granted…

Let the truth be told, whatever you are using as your substitution in life, it is just a haven to cover up in a temporary way….Cease, the bandages over life's crystallized moments that take you un expected to journeys wished & non cared for at some frivolously risk….Be cautious, of these zones, for guard yourself with the sincerity prayer…

Teddy Bears

So soft, so mushy & rather comforting as I take hold of them with my bare…

I passionate, these rather beautiful things, like there were no last, for there were creative animals that would leave a rather aliasing feeling…Teddy Bears, Teddy Bears, squeeze them once or twice & some more ….For they will never be alone….

"The Twin I never Knew"

She seemly appeared like me, same smile and facial structure of me
exact…

She even walked as me & thought as I did in every decisive way…

She lived miles away , but she in fact was brought to existence out of
the love for me…

The Vision

I saw it so clear in my sleep, what I passionately kept a beat…

It was the lyrics of the words of emotions poured from ones soul to another…

I loved the extreme make over of manifestation of how ones dictation could conclude ones destination..

I saw it, spoke it, wrote it, & proposed an evitable strategy that would have no chose but to come to life in its desirable creation….

The vision, is analyses for the crystallization of its full filling net worth…

Surely, if this burning passion, came to one yearning for more & more, it would not come to pass, but make it rightful place be known…

The Vision, traveled on so many elevations, and endured so long for the ambivalence was cured all along…..

"The Wife of Mine"

She seemly was designed with such fragile pieces, untouched indeed..

She carried herself with such magnificent integrity to ones that
looked on

Everyone smiled with a great pride, as her husband held his head
immensely high

Oh, the love of live was gratifying to thee, Oh how I loved thee, and I
am greatly delighted that you have been adjoined to me..

The wife of mine, has this yearning for me, that sends a sensational
chill down my spine, for I know she's destined for me....

"The World Owes You Nothing"

If you constantly have the motto that the world owes you something, then brace yourself for this fact that it doesn't & it want... Anything worth having, there will be some challenges along the way, but don't stop at that , just keep on moving & know the best is yet to come..

There is No Tomorrow

There are so many that give way to what tomorrow may bring in such a vast way…Not clearly understanding they have speeded times way…I live today with no regrets , for tomorrow could be in such a rare way.. I couldn't fore see the what's & where's this could bring me to be in thee…For only the heavens will know, whether tomorrow could fold….

Three Sides of the Story

We all know there, is numerous sides of the story line to analyzing to the full capacity , for we know we thought to be might not be or should I say ought of… There is his side, her side, & the truths side….Unclear just what to believe, he sounded like he could really be sincere, but then again, she sounded even more clear & honest to me….When you merged the both it became complex to others…Who was reverting the truth, him or her…You were so decisive in what to follow, your emphatic reasoning on how you came to your conclusion…

Triumphs

So many trials, so many errors in thy ways...

We feared the one thing most knew of , our challenges that faced us
face to face in everyway...

We wish to run & even hide, but never coming to realization, that we
can with stand the test to become a complete success....No one knows
where the road or journey will go, but you will never know its full
reward, if you never run this road...Triumphs in one, are far too many
to let it be wasted to another untold....

Trouble Makers

You hear them coming before you actually see them…Never knowing, what the highlight will be appearing today….Oh heck no, what did you hear them say, your name in some crazy deranged disarrayed they have plastered in everyway….You tempted to set the record straight, but you knew this was like adding fire to what was already elevated …They are ones people find themselves making excuses for why they choice not to stay in their destructive way…Make room, for this vindictive being, starting to crowd and invade ones personal space…. Use the caution , when approaching these rare zones, where nothing but evilness lays alone…..

Unexpected

So un predictable of what would sway my way…No set plan on what to sort out to do … Somewhere, I thought of the what ifs came, I would still be able to follow through on to the next…You never know, when it may come, for it approached me blindly from the start…However, since it was not intended, I have managed to accept the things that I can change, and the things that I have no control of, may it fall where it may…

Well Beyond

Beyond ones measures, consoled to one…Through this journey of effect less endeavors carried out by one…

Contempt, on being confined to the same scenario in one…

It last for well beyond this life to one, at last the time had come , for one to seek more than the last, but un measurable deeds for others and self to be won…

Well beyond , Well beyond, the love I give, the air I breathe, there were no actual words that could or would describe the well beyond theory to one…

What Came Over Me

I been waiting on you all day, mentally ravishing thoughts of us spoon hugged in thee…

Wanting to try everything kinky there was to meet…You digging it, for just wanting to explore your every compulsive snafu that I was willing and able to mold… What came over me, What came over me, I imagined you most indecisive bare exploding like the volcanoes air…. You appeared weary, for what I would dare.. Turning you inside & out without any hesitation in this dilation…

I was ready to take hold to the newest endeavor , grabbing an inch and then another, leaving you to be ..No not really just bull jiving your mental gravity in thee…You never saw it coming, for it was spontaneously , lovers exploring every measly option in thee…. What came over me, I tell you feeling my inner sexual tee…Yearning that closeness all around me…Needing you, totally, so don't you dare hold any out from me….

What is your Given Purpose

We all at some point or another have doubted your purpose on earth…

We seemly torture ourselves with un answered questions we have prearranged, to only get omit to the next…

We set out on numerous endeavors , wishing & hoping to find that something or someone to fulfill that void …

What is your given purpose, What is your given purpose, so many thoughts into this one, we asked our mothers, fathers, sisters, & even those brothers…No one really had a clear cut reasoning , on what was to be done or even to do….

What is your given purpose, It is to full fill each assignment to its fullest until the next makes itself to be known….

Surely, you would not allow your mind to set at peace with this, so don't just dwell on such, but rather, go on the assumption that the journey is full of exciting unknown zones never traveled entered into before….

What Keeps me Going

I start my daily day with a prayer of hope & peace for the inner too much more…

What keeps me going, I awake to other persons that depend heavenly on thee…

They call me mommy & wait for the thoughtful word for the day…

I would relate these words in such a meaningful way, Be a leader & not a follower to others that watch you when you call yourself being discreet…

When attempting, one assignment & the outcome may not be what I thought it ought to be….I began again, to the next task with more driven power than before….What keeps me going, I feel the energy from me to you as I hand down to you the prayer of hope that never ceases with much cause to thee….

What Point Are You At

There are lots of points in our everyday lives that follow very thin lines of no regrets..

What point are you at, Suicidal, thinking with no after regrets…Never once stopping to consider all others that surround thee….What point are you at, Confident in self, & could care less about the rest…

What point are you at, impulsive reaction , leaving a conclusive illusion of what to expect…What point are you at, living life to the fullest & never second guessing what to do or even what to say., it is alright with you….What point are you at, whatever it is , wherever it is, know that there is a friend so dear, that allots plenty of quality time to carry you through…His name is Jesus, the one that can drive you to your destined point….

What to Believe

Believe none of what you see, some of what you hear…In the end, use good judgment in understanding the difference….

Why Are you in Questioning

Why are you in such questioning of what it is or what I said so openly ,
whether rare…

You allotted too much energy, on the frivolous things that have no
special meaning in no form or way…

You place doubt of all that has been shown for thee in every detailed
way possible….Makes one wonder, where are you going with such
broad thoughts, when all that was said was straight from ones heart to
another that clearly see through the messiness of others around thee…

Why are you in questioning, when the actions have left one feeling
appreciated for all that they are and not what they can be to all…

Stop questioning, what you see & feel that lies clear for you to see….

Why are you so Cold to Me

Why are you so cold to me, is it because you grew up before it was told
to you, child how I love thee..

We never will know the depth of the pain that laid inside of thee..

As a child, I felt the wrath of neglect leaning towards me, as I reached
out for love, and not one single hand reached back to me...

Why are you so cold to me, is it that you never understood what it was
to give love to another human being that was close to thee...

Special Thanks

I was inspired to writing this poetry book, for my burning desire to share the gifted joys that god has stored in me to others. My poetry, Is my passion & joy. I wanted something reachable to others who may be or have gone through some of the dialogues in which I have spoken of.. Perhaps, it may help alleviate some of the discomforts of the transitional change in life..

I would like to thank my three beautiful kids Diamond, Desmond, & Destiny, who are my all and all in joy.. Much thanks, to my husband, Robert, who has been there no matter where my endeavors in journeys took me, but through it all he stuck it out. I give my love & appreciation to my parents, Bennie & Cynthia Rice, who instilled in me good character, love, happiness & to never limit what god has already predestined for you. I would also like to thank my other mother, Shirley Henderson, who brought me into this world and later reunited in a very special way.

Thanks, to all my siblings, Bennie Rice(Jacqueline), Latarsha Benton(Michael), Jillian Davenport(Kevin) & Lakaye Cheek for being loving in all you do. I thank every inspiring words shared throughout this process from close friends, who spoke this day into existence as if they were for certain, I had it in me.

Lastly, I thank my mentors with the company, Dianne, & others that stepped in along the way, for god knew who to place in my path so that I would get to my predestined location .

I love each of you & sincerely, hope each of you that reads this book, will be relieved, of those daily issues that may come your way.